A life-changing encounter
with God's Word from the book of

2 THESSALONIANS

*Rom 8.' 31 - What then shall we say to
these thing? If God is for us, who can be against us,*

NAVPRESS

*A NavPress resource published in alliance
with Tyndale House Publishers, Inc.*

NAVPRESS⟨⟩

NavPress is the publishing ministry of The Navigators, an international Christian organization and leader in personal spiritual development. NavPress is committed to helping people grow spiritually and enjoy lives of meaning and hope through personal and group resources that are biblically rooted, culturally relevant, and highly practical.

For more information, visit www.NavPress.com.

2 Thessalonians

Copyright © 1997, 2014 by The Navigators. All rights reserved.

A NavPress resource published in alliance with Tyndale House Publishers, Inc.

ISBN 978-0-89109-992-5

Printed in the United States of America

21   20   19   18   17   16   15
15   14   13   12   11   10   9

CONTENTS

ACKNOWLEDGMENTS

The LIFECHANGE series has been produced through the coordinated efforts of a team of Navigator Bible study developers and NavPress editorial staff, along with a nationwide network of field-testers.

AUTHOR: DIETRICH GRUEN
SERIES EDITOR: KAREN LEE-THORP

HOW TO USE THIS STUDY

Objectives

Most guides in the LIFECHANGE series of Bible studies cover one book of the Bible. Although the LIFECHANGE guides vary with the books they explore, they share some common goals:

1. To provide you with a firm foundation of understanding and a thirst to return to the book.

2. To teach you by example how to study a book of the Bible without structured guides.

3. To give you all the historical background, word definitions, and explanatory notes you need, so that your only other reference is the Bible.

4. To help you grasp the message of the book as a whole.

5. To teach you how to let God's Word transform you into Christ's image.

Each lesson in this study is designed to take sixty to ninety minutes to complete on your own. The guide is based on the assumption that you are completing one lesson per week, but if time is limited you can do half a lesson per week or whatever amount allows you to be thorough.

Flexibility

LIFECHANGE guides are flexible, allowing you to adjust the quantity and depth of your study to meet your individual needs. The guide offers many optional questions in addition to the regular numbered questions. The optional questions, which appear in the margins of the study pages, include the following:

Optional Application. Nearly all application questions are optional; we hope you will do as many as you can without overcommitting yourself.

5

For Thought and Discussion. Beginning Bible students should be able to handle these, but even advanced students need to think about them. These questions frequently deal with ethical issues and other biblical principles. They often offer cross-references to spark thought, but the references do not give obvious answers. They are good for group discussions.

For Further Study. These include: (a) cross-references that shed light on a topic the book discusses, and (b) questions that delve deeper into the passage. You can omit them to shorten a lesson without missing a major point of the passage.

If you are meeting in a group, decide together which optional questions to prepare for each lesson, and how much of the lesson you will cover at the next meeting. Normally, the group leader should make this decision, but you might let each member choose his or her own application questions.

As you grow in your walk with God, you will find the LIFECHANGE guide growing with you—a helpful reference on a topic, a continuing challenge for application, a source of questions for many levels of growth.

Overview and details

The study begins with an overview of 2 Thessalonians. The key to interpretation is context—what is the whole passage or book *about?*—and the key to context is purpose—what is the author's *aim* for the whole work? In lesson 1, you will lay the foundation for your study of 2 Thessalonians by asking yourself, *Why did the author (and God) write the book? What did they want to accomplish? What is the book about?*

Then over the next six lessons, you will analyze successive passages in detail. You'll interpret particular verses in light of what the whole paragraph is about. You'll consider how each passage contributes to the total message of the book. (Frequently reviewing a chart or outline of the book will enable you to make these connections.) Then, once you understand what the passage says, you'll apply it to your own life.

In lesson 7, you will review the whole epistle, returning to the big picture to see whether your view of it has changed after closer study. Review will also strengthen your grasp of major issues and give you an idea of how you have grown from your study.

Kinds of questions

Bible study on your own—without a structured guide—follows a progression. First you observe: What does the passage *say?* Then you interpret: What does the passage *mean?* Lastly you apply: How does this truth *affect* my life?

Some of the "how" and "why" questions will take some creative thinking, even prayer, to answer. Some are opinion questions without clear-cut right answers; these will lend themselves to discussions and side studies.

Don't let your study become an exercise in knowledge alone. Treat the passage as God's Word, and stay in dialogue with Him as you study. Pray,

"Lord, what do You want me to see here?" "Father, why is this true?" "Lord, how does this apply to my life?"

It is important that you write down your answers. The act of writing clarifies your thinking and helps you to remember what you have learned.

Study aids

A list of reference materials, including a few notes of explanation to help you make good use of them, begins on page 83. This guide is designed to include enough background to let you interpret with just your Bible and the guide. Still, if you want more information on a subject or want to study a book on your own, try the references listed.

Scripture versions

Unless otherwise indicated, the Bible quotations in this guide are from the New International Version of the Bible. Other versions cited are the Revised Standard Version (RSV) and the King James Version (KJV).

Use any translation you like for study, preferably more than one. A paraphrase such as The Living Bible is not accurate enough for study, but it can be helpful for comparison or devotional reading.

Memorizing and meditating

A psalmist wrote, "I have hidden your word in my heart that I might not sin against you" (Psalm 119:11). If you write down a verse or passage that challenges or encourages you and reflect on it often for a week or more, you will find it beginning to affect your motives and actions. We forget quickly what we read once; we remember what we ponder.

When you find a significant verse or passage, you might copy it onto a card to keep with you. Set aside five minutes during each day just to think about what the passage might mean in your life. Recite it over to yourself, exploring its meaning. Then, return to your passage as often as you can during your day, for a brief review. You will soon find it coming to mind spontaneously.

For group study

A group of four to ten people allows the richest discussions, but you can adapt this guide for other sized groups. It will suit a wide range of group types, such as home Bible studies, growth groups, youth groups, and businessmen's studies. Both new and experienced Bible students, and new and mature Christians, will benefit from the guide. You can omit or leave for later years any questions you find too easy or too hard.

The guide is intended to lead a group through one lesson per week. However, feel free to split lessons if you want to discuss them more thoroughly. Or, omit some questions in a lesson if preparation or discussion time is limited. You can always return to this guide for personal study later. You will be able to discuss only a few questions at length, so choose some for discussion and others for background. Make time at each discussion for members to ask about anything they didn't understand.

Each lesson in the guide ends with a section called "For the group." These sections give advice on how to focus a discussion, how you might apply the lesson in your group, how you might shorten a lesson, and so on. The group leader should read each "For the group" at least a week ahead so that he or she can tell the group how to prepare for the next lesson.

Each member should prepare for a meeting by writing answers for all of the background and discussion questions to be covered. If the group decides not to take an hour per week for private preparation, then expect to take at least two meetings per lesson to work through the questions. Application will be very difficult, however, without private thought and prayer.

Two reasons for studying in a group are accountability and support. When each member commits in front of the rest to seek growth in an area of life, you can pray with one another, listen jointly for God's guidance, help one another to resist temptation, assure each other that the other's growth matters to you, use the group to practice spiritual principles, and so on. Pray about one another's commitments and needs at most meetings. Spend the first few minutes of each meeting sharing any results from applications prompted by previous lessons. Then discuss new applications toward the end of the meeting. Follow such sharing with prayer for these and other needs.

If you write down each other's applications and prayer requests, you are more likely to remember to pray for them during the week, ask about them at the next meeting, and notice answered prayers. You might want to get a notebook for prayer requests and discussion notes.

Notes taken during discussion will help you to remember, follow up on ideas, stay on the subject, and clarify a total view of an issue. But don't let note-taking keep you from participating. Some groups choose one member at each meeting to take notes. Then someone copies the notes and distributes them at the next meeting. Rotating these tasks can help include people. Some groups have someone take notes on a large pad of paper or erasable marker board so that everyone can see what has been recorded.

Page 86 lists some good sources of counsel for leading group studies.

INTRODUCTION
Background to 2 Thessalonians

Map of the Roman Empire

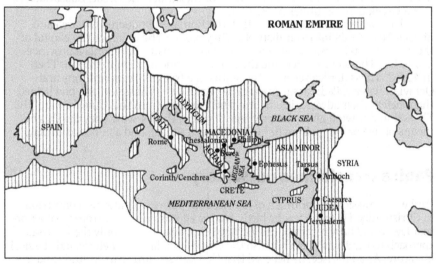

The poet Antipater called Thessalonica the "mother of all Macedon."[1] Strabo, the Greek geographer of the Augustan Age, described it as Macedonia's most populous town and the metropolis of the entire province.[2] Indeed, with a population of over 200,000, Thessalonica was widely considered a city to be reckoned with . . . economically, politically, and militarily.

When the apostle Paul traveled throughout Macedonia on his second missionary tour, he encountered a land of high mountains, broad rivers, and fertile valleys. This area of the world boasted rich farmland and timber, and was well known for its extensive deposits of silver and gold.

Thessalonica had flourished for hundreds of years, largely because of its ideal location on the banks of the Thermaic Gulf near the northwest corner

9

of the Aegean Sea. It was one of the main sea ports in the provinces of Greece and Asia, and was accordingly considered a leading shipping and naval center. Thessalonica enjoyed another advantage. The Egnatian Way, the main Roman road from Rome to the Orient via Byzantium (modern Istanbul), passed right through the city. These factors put Thessalonica in direct contact with many other important cities by both land and sea. It is no wonder that this thriving metropolis achieved commercial dominance throughout this part of the world.

A famous woman immortalized

The historical roots of Thessalonica go back to 315 BC when Cassander built it near the site of an ancient city called Therma (named for the hot springs in the area). He chose this location because of its ideal proximity to other cities. After laying the foundation of the new city, he affectionately named it after his wife, Thanica, who was a half sister of Alexander the Great. Cassander was a Greek general under Alexander.

Many years later (around 168 BC), the Romans conquered the area and divided Macedonia into four districts. They named Thessalonica the capital of the second district. Still later, when the Romans made Macedonia a province in 146 BC, Thessalonica became the seat of provincial administration. Then in 42 BC, Thessalonica received the status of a free city from Anthony and Octavian (later called Caesar Augustus) because the Thessalonians had helped them defeat their adversaries, Brutus and Cassius. From this time forward, the Thessalonians were given the privilege of ruling themselves. They did this by means of five or six "politarchs" (city rulers), a senate, and a public assembly.

Paul: a transformed missionary

Paul was a missionary for much of his life, both before and after his conversion to Christianity. He was a Jew by birth, but his education was far from what a normal Jew would have received. His learning encompassed not only the Pharisaic approach to the Jewish Law but also the Greek disciplines of rhetoric and classical literature. As a Pharisee, he believed that God had set him apart to study and live by the *Torah* (the Law of Moses), and like a good Pharisee, he expected a Man to arise who would liberate Israel from the grip of Roman domination. Accordingly, when some Jews began saying that Jesus (who obviously hadn't overthrown Rome) was this predicted Messiah, he stood against them with a vengeance!

In a sense, Saul (Paul's Jewish name) became a zealous anti-Christian missionary. His first appearance in the New Testament is that of a persecutor of the church of Jesus Christ. He officiated at the stoning of Stephen; he imprisoned every Christian he could get his hands on in Jerusalem; and he even made "missionary trips" to areas outside of Palestine to bring back believers in Christ who had fled for safety (see Acts 7:58–8:3; 9:1-2; 1 Corinthians 15:9; Philippians 3:6). His mission was to stop the spread of Christianity.

It was on such a trip to Damascus that Saul had a blinding encounter with Jesus Christ. This event, which took place around AD 35, led him to turn from Pharisaism to a devoted obedience to the living and resurrected Christ. He ended up joining those he had been persecuting! Formerly he was a missionary against the church of Christ. Now he became a missionary par excellence for the cause of Christ.

After his conversion to Christianity, Paul engaged in three great missionary tours. His second missionary tour took place around AD 49 (about fourteen years after his conversion) and brought him to several important cities, including Philippi, Thessalonica, Corinth, and Ephesus.

Paul visits Thessalonica

Upon arriving in Thessalonica, Paul began his usual activities of soul-winning and earning a livelihood. He found a friend in Jason, who was apparently one of Paul's earliest converts in the city. Jason provided his home as a base of operations for Paul and his missionary companions. Once settled, Paul probably went to work immediately making tents to earn money as he had done in other cities, for later in his letters to the Thessalonians he reminded them that he had worked "night and day in order not to be a burden to anyone while we preached the gospel of God to you" (1 Thessalonians 2:9; see 2 Thessalonians 3:8).

When the time came to preach the gospel, Paul followed his custom of first going to the local Jewish synagogue, where he knew he would find people who held a great deal in common with him: a mutual respect for the Old Testament, theological concepts, and cultural practices. In his thinking, this was where he stood the greatest chance for success. As a trained teacher, Paul was allowed to speak in the synagogue. According to Luke, his main message to the Thessalonians consisted of two points: (1) the Old Testament taught a suffering, dying, and resurrected Messiah, and (2) these predictions were fulfilled in Jesus of Nazareth.

Paul's mission met with immediate success, and many believed, both Jews and Greeks. First Thessalonians 1:9 indicates that many of his Greek converts were former idol-worshipers. Most people in the ancient world worshiped natural forces and human drives, conceived of as gods who could be portrayed in wood, stone, or metal. Sexuality was a strong feature of pagan worship, and Paul found it necessary to address this very issue in 1 Thessalonians 4:1-8. The pursuit of religious ecstasy through sex was a hard habit to break.

The core of this young church was no doubt made up of "God-fearers," a Jewish term for Greeks who attached themselves in varying degrees to the Jewish worship and way of life without as yet becoming full converts. To become a full convert involved circumcision for males, but Greeks viewed this rite as a repugnant mutilation of the body. Paul's message included all of the attractive elements of Judaism without the unattractive ones.

These God-fearers were openly dissatisfied with pagan morality and were already drawn to Jewish ethical teaching. They were also impressed by Jewish monotheism. Yet in spite of their attraction to Judaism, they disliked

11

its narrow nationalism and ritual requirements. Christianity did away with these objections, and provided a loftier concept of God as well as a nobler ethic centered in the person of Jesus Christ. Paul's Christ welcomed all races, in contrast to Jewish exclusivism. This group of Greeks provided Paul with fertile soil on which to plant the seeds of the gospel in this Thessalonian synagogue.

Persecution begins

Because many were converting from Judaism to Christianity, the Jewish leaders saw Paul's message as a serious threat. They hired troublemakers to spread false accusations about him and his associates. A mob ended up storming Jason's house. But failing to find the missionaries, the mob dragged Jason before the politarchs. Jason was charged with harboring treasonous revolutionaries. These revolutionaries were supposedly teaching the people to disobey Roman law and to follow a king other than Caesar.

The politarchs saw through the motives of these Jewish zealots and required only that Jason guarantee that the missionaries would not disturb the city's peace any longer. Paul and his friends chose to leave Thessalonica to avoid further trouble.

Paul's first letter to Thessalonica

Upon leaving Thessalonica, Paul, Silas, and Timothy proceeded about forty miles west along the Egnatian Way to Berea. They ministered in this area for a short time until some of the hostile Thessalonian Jews tracked them down and incited the Berean Jews to expel them from their city.

Paul accordingly headed for Athens while Silas and Timothy remained in Berea. After arriving in Athens, he immediately sent a message back to his companions in Berea asking them to join him, which they did (see Acts 17:10-15; 1 Thessalonians 3:1-5).

When they met up again, Paul was so concerned about the Thessalonian converts that he decided to send Timothy back to Thessalonica in order to check on their welfare. The circumstances of his hasty departure had meant his new converts would be exposed to persecution for which they were scarcely prepared. Paul simply had not had sufficient time to give them all the basic teaching he thought they required.

After revisiting Thessalonica, Timothy rejoined Paul at his next stop, Corinth, with encouraging news (see Acts 18:1,5; 1 Thessalonians 3:6-7). In spite of heavy persecution, the Thessalonians were standing strong in their new faith. But Timothy's report also indicated that they were experiencing some problems for which they needed instruction from Paul. They sent questions back to Paul via Timothy, and Paul responded by writing a letter to them from Corinth. The letter is simply addressed to "the church of the Thessalonians in God our Father and the Lord Jesus Christ."

Paul's second letter to Thessalonica

Paul's second letter quickly followed the first. Some scholars estimate that only weeks separate the two, while others believe that as many as six months had passed.[3] Not much in the recipients' situation had changed, so Paul's purpose for writing 2 Thessalonians is very much the same as for 1 Thessalonians. Paul does correct some misunderstanding about the Lord's return and the necessity of working for a living in the meantime. Eschatology (the doctrine of "last things") was a major preoccupation of the believers in Paul's day, especially those at Thessalonica. Paul devoted much of his two letters to this vital, but often puzzling, subject.

Apocalyptic expectations at Thessalonica

Interest in the end times was keen in the early church, but nowhere more so than at Thessalonica. Almost 40 percent of Paul's correspondence to the Thessalonians is devoted to the doctrine of last things.

This doctrine of last things was a source of great comfort to those living under persecution. But many wondered whether loved ones who had died would miss out on Christ's return. Paul had to assure the Thessalonians that Christ's return would coincide with the resurrection of the dead, and that all Christians would be prepared for it—not because Christians are privy to its timing, but because true believers live in a state of permanent readiness for Christ's return.[4]

In 1 Thessalonians, Paul described Christ's return as imminent, happening without warning ("like a thief in the night," 1 Thessalonians 5:2). But in 2 Thessalonians, he describes a series of events—for example, a severe tribulation and large-scale apostasy—precipitated by the "man of lawlessness," all of which must take place before the end. In effect, all Christians have ample warning if they read the signs marking the "beginning of the end."

The leader of this large-scale apostasy is known as the "man of lawlessness" (2 Thessalonians 2:3), the "antichrist" (1 John 2:18), the "abomination that causes desolation" (Daniel 9:27; Matthew 24:15), "false messiahs" (Mark 13:22), and the "beast" (see Revelation 13:1-10). Two prototypes in history lie behind these images of the Antichrist: Antiochus Epiphanes (ruled 175–164 BC); and Emperor Gaius, also known as Caligula (ruled AD 37–41). Both demanded the worship reserved only for the one true and living God (see Daniel 11:36; 2 Thessalonians 2:4).

Lesser "antichrists" and "false messiahs" have been paving the way for the final Antichrist ever since. This Antichrist was understood in Jewish and Christian thought to be either a persecuting tyrant of Rome, the incarnation of Belial (see 2 Corinthians 6:15), a false prophet (see 1 John 4:1-3), a Jew, or even one of many regional enemies of Israel (see Isaiah 10:12-19; 14:4-21; Ezekiel 28:2-10).

When Christ returns in glory, this great rebel will be destroyed. Until then, the Antichrist or man of lawlessness will be restrained from full-scale evil (see 2 Thessalonians 2:6-7), perhaps by imperial Rome.[5] On this particular wording, scholar F. F. Bruce adds, "Even after the Roman Empire passed away, [this interpretation] did not become obsolete, for when the secular power in any form continues to discharge its divinely ordained commission, it restrains evil and prevents the outburst of anarchy."[6]

Relation between the two letters

The two letters assume such similar circumstances in their audiences that they must have been sent out within a short interval of each other. The overlap between 1 and 2 Thessalonians is redundant at many points, and yet the eschatological outlook differs remarkably between the two. This raises questions about their relation to one another.

Why would a second, largely redundant, letter be needed so soon after the first? Could it be that each letter went to a distinct segment of the church, even two churches at Thessalonica—perhaps 1 Thessalonians to Gentile Christians (who have "turned to God from idols," 1 Thessalonians 1:9), and 2 Thessalonians to Jewish Christians? Or could it be that both letters were sent at the same time, not to the same church at Thessalonica, but rather one to a different church in Macedonia—perhaps Berea or Philippi (in the latter event, yielding "1 and 2 Philippians")? The answer is wrapped up in the second question.

Which letter actually came first? The traditional New Testament sequence of Pauline letters (from Romans through Philemon) is based on length, not date. And 1 Thessalonians is almost twice the length of 2 Thessalonians, so it is placed first, but nothing in either letter requires that one precede the other. The arguments for the priority of 2 Thessalonians are chiefly these:[7]

1. The recipients of 2 Thessalonians are said to be currently suffering persecution (see 1:4-5), whereas 1 Thessalonians refers to persecution in the past tense (see 2:14).
2. The deplorable idleness of some church members has just come to the writer's attention, prompting his reply in 2 Thessalonians (see 3:11-12), whereas this welfare mentality is a well-known fact to the writers and readers of 1 Thessalonians (see 4:10-12; 5:14).
3. The personal signature at the end of 2 Thessalonians (see 3:17) is meaningful only if this is the first letter to the addressees. The addressees, presumably, would not need such an explanatory footnote if this were the second letter from Paul.
4. The two sections of 1 Thessalonians that begin with "now about" (4:9; 5:1) may well be reconsidering topics already taken up in 2 Thessalonians: "love for one another" (1 Thessalonians 4:9, compare 2 Thessalonians 1:3) and "times and dates" (1 Thessalonians 5:1, compare 2 Thessalonians 2:1-12).

Against these arguments, the priority of 1 Thessalonians can be asserted:

1. The readers of 2 Thessalonians may be in receipt of a previous letter (see 2:15), whereas 1 Thessalonians makes no such reference to a previous letter.

14

2. The teaching in 2 Thessalonians 2:1-12 looks like a correction to believers who anticipated Christ's imminent return.

1. F. Jacobs, *Anthology Graecae*, vol. 2, no. 14, p. 98. Cited in Merrill F. Unger, *Archaeology and the New Testament* (Grand Rapids, MI: Zondervan, 1962), 226.
2. Strabo, vol. 7, paragraphs 323 and 330. Compare Harold R. Willoughby, "Archaeology and Christian Beginnings," *Biblical Archaeology*, vol. 3 (September 1939), 32–33. Cited in Unger, 226.
3. Ronald A. Ward, *Commentary on 1 & 2 Thessalonians* (Waco, TX: Word, 1973), 127.
4. F. F. Bruce, *1 & 2 Thessalonians* (Waco, TX: Word, 1982), xxxvi–xxxix, 179–188.
5. Bruce, 188.
6. Bruce, 188.
7. Bruce, xli–xlii.

Jan 13, 16

OVERVIEW OF 2 THESSALONIANS

Imagine receiving a letter from a trusted friend, one who has been through what you're going through and is offering valuable advice. You might take several approaches to the letter. You may read it through quickly, looking for first impressions and any news. You then read it a second time, taking time to savor it. After setting it aside, you may read it a third time, with pen in hand for note-taking and a considered response.

This overview lesson is like that. It asks you to read and reread this brief letter several times, each time with a different purpose or approach.

First impressions

1. a. Read through 2 Thessalonians quickly, looking for the overall message and first impressions. Is there any good news worth shouting about?

_____

_____

_____

b. Any bad news worth watching out for?

_____

_____

it took so long to get the letter. We shall meet up in the air Jesus Christ is coming back that we knew.

God the son / God the Holy Spirit / God the Father

Love Omniscient

Just / merciful / Creator

Judge / Sovereign /

Omnipotent / Faithful

God is a Good God

God is enchange.

Prays in a Praise

intensin —

spirit glaa —

application —

We need to under- stand / one of these days will be the end.

17

_____

_____

_____

c. Any concerns to pray about?

_____

_____

_____

_____

d. What other reactions or impressions do you have after reading it?

_____

_____

_____

2. a. Read Paul's letter again, this time more slowly. What do you notice about his mood? (Is he hopeful? Formal? Concerned? Thankful? Stern?)

_____

_____

_____

b. Do you detect any shifts in mood? (Where? Why?)

_____

_____

_____

_____

3. Think about how Paul communicates his message. How would you describe the style or delivery of this letter? (Sermonic? Argumentative? Personal?)

_____

_____

_____

_____

_____

_____

_____

_____

4. a. Repetition, or how often an author uses certain words or phrases, gives a clue to the author's intent in writing a letter. What words or phrases occur over and over? (Hint: Don't get hung up on the exact wording used, as this may vary from translation to translation. Instead go for broad themes.)

_____

_____

_____

_____

_____

b. What main themes or topics are suggested by these repeated words?

_____

_____

_____

_____

_____

_____

Broad outline

5. Read through 2 Thessalonians a third time (preferably in a different translation). Think of a short sentence that captures the main point or gives a title to paragraph divisions or other bite-size Scripture portions. The first one is done for you. (Paragraph divisions, even verse numbers and sentence punctuation, were not in the original Greek or Hebrew manuscripts, but were added centuries later for ease of reading. The divisions in your Bible may differ from the ones given here.)

   After titling the smaller portions, give an overall title to each chapter or main block of Scripture.

1:1-12 _____

_____

   1:1-2 Paul, Silas, and Timothy greet believers at Thessalonica

   1:3-4 _____

_____

   1:5-7a _____

_____

   1:7b-10 _____

_____

   1:11-12 _____

_____

2:1-17 _____

_____

   2:1-2 _____

_____

20

2:3-8 _____

_____

2:9-10 _____

_____

2:11-12 _____

_____

2:13-15 _____

_____

2:16-17 _____

_____

3:1-18 _____

_____

3:1-2 _____

_____

3:3-5 _____

_____

3:6-10 _____

_____

3:11-15 _____

_____

3:16-18 _____

_____

After doing this outline procedure on your own,
compare your outlines with each other and with
the sample outline and chart provided (see pages
26 and 27). There is no single correct answer, so
discuss in your group why you prefer one sentence
summary over another.

Study Skill—Outlining

Outlining a passage will sharpen your focus and increase your retention of its main points. Outlining also helps us capture the flow or train of thought in the book. If it appears some points are subordinate to others, or if some points are mere particulars in relation to a larger general point, you can indicate that in your outline by using capital letters or Roman numerals for main points, and letters or numbers for secondary points. (If you see that the author digresses somewhere to make a sidebar comment, you can indicate that point with parentheses.) The outline below[1] is provided as a sample.

I.   Greeting from Paul, Silas, and Timothy (1:1-2)

II. Doctrine as Ground of Encouragement and Challenge (1:3–2:17)

   A. The Doctrine of Vindication (1:3-12)
     1. Thanksgiving an obligation (1:3-4)
     2. Fidelity and encouragement (1:5-10)
     3. Prayer a consequence (1:11-12)
   B. The Doctrine of the Second Advent (2:1-17)
     1. The keynote: no alarm (2:1-2)
     2. The order of events (2:3-5)
     3. Secret activity temporarily restrained (2:6-7)
     4. . . .
     5. . . .

III. Misbehavior as an Occasion for Admonition (3:1-16)

   A. Request for Prayer (3:1-2)
   B. Statement of Confidence (3:3-5)
     1. In the Lord (3:3)
     2. . . .
     3. . . .

6. Drawing from your own first impressions and outline summaries, what do you think was Paul's purpose(s) for writing this letter? (Hint: Wherever the author pauses to address his audience as "brothers and sisters," he is accenting a main point.)

1:3 _____

_____

2:1-2 _____

_____

2:13 _____

_____

2:15 _____

_____

_____

3:1 _____

_____

_____

3:6 _____

_____

_____

Overall theme _____

_____

_____

7. If you have not already done so, read the historical background on pages 9–15 of this study guide. Did the introductory material get you to rethink some of your presumptions about the text? Explain.

_____

_____

_____

_____

_____

_____

8. In your readings of 2 Thessalonians, what concepts did you come across that you are curious about and will warrant further study in the weeks to come? Jot down your questions below. (Some of your questions may be answered later in this study guide. The resources listed on pages 83–87 may help you answer the tougher questions.)

_____

_____

_____

_____

_____

_____

_____

Your response

9. What does your group have in common with the original readers and hearers of 2 Thessalonians? (Note: Readers today might have a different purpose for studying the letter than the author had in addressing his original readers.)

_____

_____

24

_____

_____

_____

_____

10. Of all the things Paul was telling his audience
    to do, what could God be leading you and your
    group to do in the next several weeks? (See the
    "For the group" section.)

_____

_____

_____

_____

_____

For the group

Warm-up. The beginning of a new group study is
a good time to lay a proper foundation for honest
sharing of personal goals and concerns, as well as
insights from your Bible study. One way to establish
common ground is to share what each member
hopes to get out of this study of 2 Thessalonians.
As you take several minutes to share your hopes
and expectations, have someone write them down.
Weeks from now you can look back at these goals to
see if they are being met.

Discussion. Take turns sharing some of your "first
impressions" (questions 1–4 in this lesson). Sharing
from your notes will help members get comfortable
with each other, and establish common ground for
your study.

  Likewise, take several minutes sharing your
sentence summaries or titles (question 5), as well as
any comparisons and insights gained from looking
at the 2 Thessalonians chart on pages 26 and 27.

Don't try to harmonize all your answers, but discuss your differences. Learn why you prefer one sentence summary over another.

Consider the occasion or purpose of this letter (questions 6 and 7). What difficult concepts would the original readers and hearers of 2 Thessalonians have readily understood, but which you will need more time and in-depth study to understand (question 8)? Take your last ten minutes to share concerns. This input will affect how your group should pace future studies.

Wrap-up. Pray about how your group will blend your different strengths and backgrounds. Some of you will have strong analytic skills, others of you will be good at facilitating group discussion, or driving home a point of application. Give thanks that God has put your group together and be willing to help each other. Don't be embarrassed to give and request help. That's why you're studying this as a group, and not just as individuals.

How you divide the time spent in individual and group study will vary according to the group size and purpose, your members' familiarity with Bible study methods, the willingness of group members to do homework, and the optional questions in the margins. The number of weeks you want to spend on the overall book study will also guide the decision on how to pace the group.

A good rule of thumb for this opening overview study is to allot twenty minutes for individual study and note-taking, and twenty minutes for sharing your first impressions and outline summaries. The remainder of your hour can be spent in reviewing individual expectations and setting group goals.

This timeline assumes you assigned the "How to Use This Study" and the "Introduction" material as homework prior to this group session. If not, you will need another twenty minutes to review that.

Chart of 2 Thessalonians

Purpose: To encourage believers to persevere in faith, loving others as Christ did, working diligently, resisting evil, and hoping in the Lord's return—all so that believers might be worthy of and sure of God's calling.

1:1-12   The Lord's Return Gives Impetus for Christian Growth
     1:1-2   Paul, Silas, and Timothy greet believers at Thessalonica
     1:3-4   Thessalonians are growing in faith and love, amidst trials
     1:5-7a   God's judgments are right and just and merciful
     1:7b-10   Unbelief and disobedience will be punished at the Lord's return
     1:11-12   Those worthy of God's calling glorify Jesus by their faith

2:1-17   A Misunderstanding About the Lord's Return
     2:1-2   The Lord has not already come and passed them by
     2:3-8   Blasphemous "man of lawlessness" is revealed and restrained
     2:9-10   Satan deceives those who refuse the truth about Christ
     2:11-12   God uses the big "lie" to punish unbelief and wickedness
     2:13-15   Those loved, chosen, and saved by God's Spirit obey the truth
     2:16-17   God's grace stirs up hope, faith, and love

3:1-18   A Lifestyle Befitting the Lord's Return
     3:1-2   Paul asks prayer for deliverance from faithless, evil people
     3:3-5   God protects us from the Evil One
     3:6-10   Paul condemns idleness, exemplifies what it means to work
     3:11-15   Paul warns against idle busybodies
     3:16-18   Paul extends grace and peace from Christ

1. Excerpted and adapted from Ronald A. Ward, *Commentary on 1 & 2 Thessalonians* (Waco, TX: Word, 1973), 131.

Jan 20, 16 we need to stay in unified. there joy in serving for God, in our weakness He is strong.
Satin
there is power of Gods justice, we love each other.

LESSON TWO   *Rev 11; 13-19 / 18; 4-8 / 20; 7*

2 THESSALONIANS 1:1-12

Good Works Worthy of God's Calling

Paul thanked God for it all. Paul was not boastful about his works, need to wait on God — His will, God will bring Justin in His timing. live your life for God.

To encourage and challenge his audience to do good works worthy of God's calling, Paul lays a ground-work of sound doctrine. He builds his case with evidence of what the Thessalonians are already doing. His call to persevere in their suffering is based on God's faithfulness to His just standards and purposes. In the end, evil deeds will be punished and good works will be rewarded. Thanksgiving for God's gifts, obedience to the gospel, and prayer for God's glory are the proper responses to what God has done and will do on our behalf.

Ask God to concentrate your focus for this study, on your own and as a group.

A faith worth boasting about (1:1-7)

1. Who are the three writers of 2 Thessalonians?

Paul _____

_____

_____

Silas *he helped Paul and* _____

_____

29

_____

_____

_____

_____

Timothy *helped Paul with churches youngly*

_____

_____

_____

_____

_____

_____

Silas (1:1). Also known as Silvanus, this frequent companion of Paul's was a leader in the Jerusalem church (see Acts 15:22), a prophet (see 15:32), and a Roman citizen (see 16:37).

Timothy (1:1). A convert and protégé of Paul's (see Acts 16:1-3; 1 Corinthians 4:17), Timothy helped Paul and Silas found the church at Thessalonica (see Acts 17:1-14; 1 Thessalonians 3:2).

God our Father (1:1). The expression implies the doctrine of adoption and the experience of intimate fellowship, whereas "God the Father" (see 1 Thessalonians 1:1) implies a note of detachment, appropriate for discussing the fatherhood of God with nonbelievers, who do not know Him as "our" Father.

Brothers and sisters (1:3; also 2:1,13,15; 3:1,6). United by Christ to each other in the family of God. This term is used more than twenty times in the Thessalonian correspondence.[1]

Ought always to thank (1:3; also 2:13). It is God's will to thank Him in all circumstances (see 1 Thessalonians 5:18). The writers' hearts were filled with gratitude because of news that the church they had founded was doing so well, against all odds. The writers also saw in the health and growth of this church a specific answer to their prayers (see 1 Thessalonians 3:12), and thus a reason for thanksgiving.

Faith . . . love . . . is increasing (1:3). Faith grows in response to God's Word. Love grows as it exercises deeper thoughtfulness, greater imagination, and wider application. Growth in these two moral virtues, which at one time were lacking in this church, also represent a direct answer to Paul's prayer (see 1 Thessalonians 3:2,6-7,10,12). Living by faith (see 2 Thessalonians 1:3-4,10-11; 2:10-12; 3:1-2) and showing love for one another are central themes of 2 Thessalonians.

Study Skill—Observation
When you study the Bible, your first step will be to make observations and write them down. A good tool for observing everything that is going on in the passage, even things that seem trivial, is the so-called W questions—Who? What? When? Where? Why?—and How? You will find examples of those questions throughout this study guide.

---

2. a. What is it about the Thessalonians' faith that makes it right for Paul to part from his usual practice and boast about this church (see 1:3-4)?

it is visible,

_____

_____

_____

b. What qualifies a church for this praiseworthy "honor roll"?

they stod fast faith. they were growing.

_____

_____

31

Therefore . . . we boast (1:4). Boasting about anything or anyone other than the Lord was contrary to apostolic practice (see Romans 3:27; 1 Corinthians 1:29-31; 3:21; 4:7; 2 Corinthians 10:17; Galatians 6:14), yet Paul knows that worthy human achievements also need recognition and magnify the grace of God.

Your perseverance and faith (1:4). Steadfastness and faith are linked, conveying the sense that steadfastness and faith are one, which no amount of persecutions and trials (see 1:4) can shake.

Study Skill—Connective Words
Connective words or phrases—such as *according to, for, therefore, in order that, if . . . then, however,* and *but*—are clues that tell you how statements relate to each other. When you see a "therefore" or a "for" introducing a clause, always ask yourself, "What is it there for?"

---

3. a. What difficulties were the Thessalonians experiencing (see 1:5-6)?

_____

_____

_____

_____

b. How does Paul encourage them (see 1:6-7a)?

God will repay with
Tribulation those troubl...

_____

_____

_____

God's judgment is right . . . God is just (1:5-6). The rightness of God's judgment is evident in that He provides the resources to inspire and sustain our faith until Judgment Day, when we enter fully into the kingdom of God and are counted worthy. Those who have trusted Christ to pay the penalty for sin are declared righteous. Those who haven't endured, but persist in their unbelief and disobedience, are punished. Either way, God's justice will be evident to all.

For Thought and Discussion: How can you tell when you are persecuted for the sake of the gospel, and when you are persecuted for something else (an attitude, decision, or character trait)?

4. a. What kind of "reward" will those who suffer for Christ's sake receive?

eternal life.

_____

_____

_____

b. When?

This will happen when flaming fire, Jesus comes at the end.

_____

When the Lord Jesus is revealed (1:7). There are three New Testament words used for this revelation or Second Coming: *apocalypse, parousia,* and *epiphany.* The word here is *apocalypse,* which means an unveiling or disclosure of something that was previously hidden, unseen, or unknown.[2] Currently, Christ is "hidden" in heaven, but that will end when God reveals Him from heaven.

In blazing fire (1:7). Flaming fire, symbolizing God's holiness, frequently accompanied divine revelation. God is a "consuming fire" (Deuteronomy 4:24; Hebrews 12:29). This fire took many forms: a burning bush on Mount Sinai (see Exodus 3:2), a continuous pillar of fire in the wilderness, and as tongues of fire at Pentecost (see Acts 2:3). Fire is also a figure of punishment and Judgment Day, as in the prophecies of Isaiah (see Isaiah 1:31; 33:11-14; 34:9-10; 66:15) and the Revelation of John (see Revelation 1:14).

With his powerful angels (1:7). Angels are witnesses who inspire faith much like the martyrs or heroes of the faith who encouraged Hebrew Christians to persevere under severe persecution (see Hebrews 12:1). As agents of God, angels have the mighty task of separating the wicked from the righteous (see Matthew 13:39-42,47-50).

Angels

Angels are ethereal spirits, but take bodily form as needed to fulfill an assignment. Contrary to some beliefs, angels are not gods, ghosts, spirits of the dead, or people who have gone to heaven. Angels are described as "messengers," "sons of God," and "holy ones" more than 300 times in both the Old and New Testaments.

In the Old Testament, for example, an angel guarded the tree from Adam and Eve in the garden (see Genesis 3:24); intervened when Abraham was about to kill Isaac (see Genesis 22:11); wrestled with Jacob (see Genesis 32:24-28); intercepted Balaam, who couldn't see the angel (see Numbers 22:23-31); saved Daniel's three friends in the fiery furnace (see Daniel 3:28); and saved Daniel from the lions' den (see Daniel 6:22).

In the New Testament, angels attended Jesus' birth (see Luke 1–2), ministered to Jesus and others in their suffering (see Hebrews 1:5-14), and worship Jesus in heavenly glory (see Revelation 5:11). Given free will, some angels fall from God's grace, like Satan (see Isaiah 14:12-14; Daniel 10:11-14; 2 Peter 2:4; Jude 6).

In Martin Luther's day (around AD 1500), churchmen divided the angels into nine groups, each with its own assignment: *seraphim* and *cherubim* worship God, *thrones* bring justice, *dominions* regulate life in heaven, *virtues* work miracles, *powers* protect us from evil, *principalities* protect the welfare of nations, *archangels* guide people, and *angels* are messengers.

Disobedience worthy of punishment

(1:8-12)

For Thought and
Discussion: Do
names today tell us
about a person's char-
acter? How?

5. a. For whom is this "punishment" or divine
wrath intended (see 1:6,8-9)?

*Sinner — Those who don't
obey*

b. Why is the punishment right for them and
not for the Thessalonians?

Study Skill—Cross-References
Parallel or similar passages of Scripture, called
cross-references, can often shed light on what
you are studying. Paul himself makes reference to a previous letter (see 2:15)—in effect, a
cross-reference to 1 Thessalonians, permitting
us to use the theology of the first letter to interpret the second. Using Scripture to interpret
Scripture is key for doing word studies.

Punish . . . punished (1:8-9). Some psychology
experts theorize that punishment has deter-
rent value only, protecting society by "making
an example" of the offender. Others believe
that punishment also has educational value
in reforming the wrongdoer. Still others argue
that punishment is primarily retribution or
repayment (not revenge) for those who do
wrong. This understanding of punishment fits
what is going on here at the final judgment,
where deterrence and education have no place.[3]

Those who do not know God (1:8). This refers to
those who have heard the gospel, but choose
not to obey it.

35

Barb
Chevy
Betty
Jeff Steve
Friday

Everlasting destruction (1:9). This destruction (complete ruin, or "hell") is as everlasting as eternal life (see Matthew 25:46). For this reason, destruction of the nonbeliever cannot mean annihilation.[4] Destruction is exclusion from the Lord's presence.

6. Given the extreme pressures that weigh upon the Thessalonians, what do Paul and his associates pray for (see 1:11-12)?

work of faith & Prover Hir goodness

Name (1:12). More than an appellation or personal label, a name in ancient cultures conveyed a person's character. Paul yearns for all glory to be given to Christ for all that He will do in and through the Thessalonian Christians.

Your response

7. A faith worth boasting about is a faith worth imitating. What can you and your group do to keep your faith growing and your conduct worthy of the kingdom?

8. How do your own ideas about hell compare with Paul's description?

_____

_____

_____

_____

_____

Study Skill—Seeing the Big Picture
Although a particular doctrinal teaching ("hell is forever") may be inferred from one verse, that inference must be confirmed by clear teaching elsewhere in the whole of Scripture. When we search the Scriptures for an overall eschatology ("doctrine of last things"), we see that the "fires of hell" burn eternally without consuming or annihilating anyone, but leave the wicked "weeping and gnashing [their] teeth" (Matthew 8:12) and wishing to warn their family about this "place of torment" (see Luke 16:23-28). We also see in Jesus' teaching that hell is an everlasting exclusion from God's presence (see Matthew 7:23).

9. a. How does the prayer agenda of your group compare with Paul's team and their prayers for the church at Thessalonica?

_____

_____

_____

_____

_____

b. If your prayers were to focus on "every good purpose," acts of faith, Christ's glory, and

37

God's grace, what would your corporate
prayers sound like? Make a list.

_____

_____

_____

_____

_____

10. Do you have any unanswered questions about
1:1-12? Write them below.

_____

_____

_____

_____

_____

For the group

Warm-up. For openers, have group members pick
one of these optional questions:

1. Whose endurance of trials and suffering, which
   resulted in eventual triumph, has inspired you
   to endure pain for gain?
2. What calling did you once aspire to "when you
   grew up"?
3. What hero did you want to know or become like?

Discussion. For a one-hour study, read 2 Thessalonians
1:1-12 and work your way through the questions on
your own. Take twenty to twenty-five minutes for
this. Regather as a group and spend another twenty
to twenty-five minutes discussing your answers.
This will be the typical time allotment for future
group sessions. However, if you have ninety minutes
at your disposal, or if you choose to do the individual study as homework before coming to group, you
can take longer to discuss questions in the group.

Paul's testimony, which was tantamount to simply preaching the gospel, encouraged the Thessalonians in their faith (see 1:10). For a follow-up to this study, and as a way to encourage commitment in your group, consider sharing your personal testimonies. These should not be more than three to five minutes long. If you allow no more than two persons per week to share their respective stories of coming to Christ, this is quite manageable within most small-group settings. Assign these testimonies a week ahead of time, so that individuals will have time outside of group to prepare. Your testimony may look like this:

1. Use an introduction that grabs attention or builds intrigue, such as "foreshadowing" (giving a clue or hint of how your story unravels or winds up) or appealing to a common felt need ("I came to college looking for love in all the wrong places").
2. Comment briefly about your past way of life. Focus on root problems, not on the blow-by-blow details or symptoms of each problem.
3. Comment briefly on what it was about Christ that first attracted you to Him, and what later convinced you of your need for Christ. Keep your testimony Christ-centered, not I-centered. Focus on felt needs that are relevant to or common to your audience. If you came to Christ at an early age ("too early to remember"), then pinpoint a time when Jesus Christ became most meaningful to you.
4. Comment briefly about your present walk with Christ. Mention one struggle for every success you highlight. Bring it up to the present day.
5. Close by reciting a relevant Scripture and asking a pointed question or two ("Have you personally trusted Christ, or are you somewhere along the way?" "Would you say you 'know God' personally, or is your faith based more on 'knowledge about God'?").

1. Leon Morris, "1 & 2 Thessalonians," *The NIV Study Bible* (Grand Rapids, MI: Zondervan, 1985), 1821.
2. Ronald A. Ward, *Commentary on 1 & 2 Thessalonians* (Waco, TX: Word, 1973), 142–143.
3. Ward, 145.
4. Morris, 1828.

LESSON THREE

2 THESSALONIANS 2:1-10a

The Day of the Lord

(handwritten, top right margin) God is coming to judge, Jesus is coming back, be coming back, IS 27:12, day of the Lord is the, day of visitation ?, it is good to find our jdgmt

To impatient children, once-a-year birthdays seem too few and far away. The words "Not yet" or "You'll have to wait" are inconceivable and intolerable. So they experiment with what theologians call an "over-realized eschatology" and claim with every passing milestone, "I'm old enough now," or "It's here already!"

The Christians at Thessalonica were like that, always thinking the Second Coming or the Day of the Lord was right around the corner. They kept asking, "Are we there yet?" Paul had to correct this misunderstanding of the Lord's timetable, so he gave the Thessalonians a list of preliminary events that would take place before the Lord's return.

The Day of the Lord (2:1-4)

1. What had the Thessalonians seen or heard that affected their emotional state or mental framework regarding the Second Coming (see 2:1-2)?

(handwritten answer) not to be shaken in mind or troubled, neither either by spirit or by word or by letter

41

For Thought and
Discussion: What
reported sightings
or prophecies (for
example, "the end is
near" or "the Christ
has come") have
you seen or heard in
newsletters or books,
from TV preachers or
cult leaders? *the
christ end is near,
some of the things
that says in Revelation
is coming to pass.*

The coming of our Lord Jesus Christ (2:1). The
word used here is *parousia* (see 1:7 and related
note). This Advent is linked to our being gathered
to Him, which suggests the author was thinking
of one combined event—that at the climax of
history Christ would not be without His church
and the church would not be without her Lord.

Gathered to him (2:1). The Greek word for "gathered" is *episunagogee*, from whose root we derive
the word synagogue. *Episunagogee* occurs only
one other place in the New Testament, where
the writer reminds believers to "meet together,"
a habit which is to be repeated "all the more as
you see the Day approaching" (Hebrews 10:25).
In context, this habit implies that gathering
for church and small-group community life is
almost a mini-version or dress rehearsal of when
Christ will gather us together at His return. Paul
speaks of believers "being gathered," implying
that this ultimate meeting is something Christ
and His angels will do for us (see 1 Thessalonians
4:17; compare Matthew 24:31; Mark 13:27).[1]

Unsettled or alarmed (2:2). The first word translates
saluo apo nous, which literally means "shaken out
of one's mind." This word implies a panic attack,
instability, or being at wit's end. Elsewhere this
word pictures a ship cut adrift of its moorings.[2]
The second word, translated "alarmed," implies
despondency and a troubled spirit, even wailing.

The day of the Lord (2:2). Rumors were flying that
this Day had already come. The full force of this
disturbing rumor on the believers at Thessalonica
was this: Not only had the Day come, but the events
of 1 Thessalonians had come—and gone—leaving
them behind.[3] This rumor had a different impact
on believers at Corinth, where certain members
embraced the kingdom of Christ as already come,

42

which they took as a signal that they themselves were reigning over others as "kings" with Him (see 1 Corinthians 4:8). Paul had a different antidote for each misunderstanding of this great Day.

2. a. How does Paul reassure the Thessalonians that Christ has not yet returned?

Some events have not come yet.

_____

_____

_____

b. What warning does he give them with his encouragement?

_____

_____

_____

_____

For Thought and Discussion: Can the teaching of a sudden return of the Lord ("like a thief in the night," 1 Thessalonians 5:2) and the teaching of a delayed or gradual return (see 2 Thessalonians 2:1-12) both be true? How?

The rebellion occurs (2:3). Widespread apostasy, instigated by the man of lawlessness, connotes either political revolt (for example, the Jewish revolt against Rome) or a religious defection (from customary doctrine, even the Law of Moses, as in Acts 21:21; or from the gospel itself, as in 1 Thessalonians 2:15-16).[4]

The man of lawlessness (2:3). The leader of this world-wide rebellion was lawless (see 2:9), not in the sense of having no knowledge of moral law, but in the sense of acting contrary to the known will of God. This person epitomizes self-exaltation, proclaiming himself to be God (see 2:4), which is the very essence of sin.[5] Hence, the variant reading, "man of sin," is quite appropriate. Another equivalent term is the "Antichrist." For more on apocalyptic expectations of the Thessalonians, see the Introduction.

For Further Study:
For biblical prec-
edents of those who
set themselves up as
objects of worship,
see Isaiah 2:11-18;
14:12-20; Ezekiel
28:2-10; and Daniel
11:36-45.

3. What does Paul say will happen before the Lord
returns (see 2:3)?

_____

_____

_____

_____

_____

_____

The man doomed to destruction (2:3). This same
term, translated "son of perdition" (RSV), was
applied to Judas Iscariot (see John 17:12), who
betrayed Jesus and later committed suicide.

He will oppose (2:4). The Greek word *antikimenos*
(meaning "adversary") was applied elsewhere to
Satan, the supreme adversary (see 1 Timothy
5:15). But here *antikimenos* cannot be Satan,
who is distinct from the lawless person (see
2 Thessalonians 2:9).

In God's temple (2:4). Figurative of the place of
God, not restricted to the temple at Jerusalem
or some denominational building or church.

The "man of lawlessness" is restrained

(2:5-10a)

4. a. Many theories have been put forth about who
is "holding back" the man of lawlessness.
Which do you find most convincing?

☐ The Roman state embodied by its emperor,
who kept the peace
☐ The preaching of the gospel to Gentiles,
especially through Paul
☐ The second Jewish state with leaders such
as James of Jerusalem
☐ The principle of law and order that holds
anarchy in check

☐ The Holy Spirit working through the state or the church
☐ Angelic powers working through the state or the church
☐ God Himself working through the state or the church
☐ Some other combination of the above

_____

_____

_____

b. What supports your answer?

_____

_____

_____

_____

What is holding him back . . . the one who now holds it back (2:6-7). The grammar allows for this restraining force to be either a thing (the gender of the participial verb is neuter in 2:6) or a person (the masculine singular pronoun in 2:7).

5. a. How will the man of lawlessness be restrained (see 2:6-7)?

_____

_____

_____

_____

_____

b. For how long?

Till He is taken away

_____

For Further Study:
What is the nature of this secret power or "mystery" in Paul's thinking? See Romans 11:25; 16:25; 1 Corinthians 2:1-7; 4:1; 13:2; 14:2; 15:51; Ephesians 1:9; 3:3-9; 5:32; 6:19; Colossians 1:26-27; 2:2; 4:3; 1 Timothy 3:16.

For Thought and Discussion: With currency and coinage it might seem easy to pick out the real from the counterfeit. How can you tell the difference between the miracles, signs, and wonders of Satan and those of God?

Secret power (2:7). Literally, "mystery," which is usually associated in the New Testament with some aspect of the gospel—specifically, the Incarnation, the death of Christ, the inclusion of Jews and Gentiles in the kingdom, and the resurrection body. This mystery is not something known only to the initiated, as in Gnosticism, which was popular in Paul's day, but is something formerly hidden and now revealed only by God.[6]

6. What will Christ accomplish "by the splendor of his [second] coming" (2:8)?

_____

_____

_____

_____

_____

The splendor of his coming (2:8). See 1:7 and related note. Two of the words associated with the Second Coming are used here: *epiphany* (translated "splendor") and *parousia* (translated "coming"). When the second coming of Christ overtakes the coming of the lawless one, the power of the Evil One is no match for the splendor of Christ.

7. What evidence is there of Satan's powerful work through the man of lawlessness (see 2:9-10a)?

_____

_____

_____

_____

_____

_____

_____

Optional Application: In light of all the current events (bad news and good news), what powers of lawlessness do you see being unleashed on the world? What agencies of God do you see at work restraining evil from getting out of hand?

Your response

8. a. How have you reacted to predictions of Christ's return in the past?

_____

_____

_____

_____

b. Has this lesson about the end times changed how you will react to similar predictions in the future?

_____

_____

_____

_____

9. a. In light of everything Paul said here about the events to come, do you think the end is near at hand, or far away?

_____

_____

_____

b. How does that affect your mindset and behavior in the meantime?

_____

_____

_____

_____

_____

10. Do you believe accounts of so-called miracles? Why, or why not?

_____

_____

_____

_____

_____

_____

For the group

Warm-up. This week's study gets to the heart of Paul's message to the Thessalonians. Begin this lesson by asking one of these questions:

1. When have you or a loved one felt "left behind," overwhelmed by that "home alone" feeling of panic? How were you able to come to terms with and understand what was happening around you?
2. When have you had to carefully reconstruct the sequence of events for someone who was trying to figure out "how long until we get there?"

Discussion. After your individual study, come together as a group to share and confirm your

48

understandings and biblical insights. This safeguards the objective truth of God's Word by hedging against the tendency of go-it-alone Christians (and cult members) to push "private interpretations" which deviate from the truth. Your goal is to cultivate a "love for truth."

Prayer. As a group, thank God for the truths about His character He has revealed in the Bible. Pray that God will enable you to persevere and live godly lives as you wait for the Lord's return.

1. Ronald A. Ward, *Commentary on 1 & 2 Thessalonians* (Waco, TX: Word, 1973), 153.
2. Leon Morris, "1 & 2 Thessalonians," *The NIV Study Bible* (Grand Rapids, MI: Zondervan, 1985), 1829.
3. F. F. Bruce, *1 & 2 Thessalonians* (Waco, TX: Word, 1982), 154.
4. Bruce, 166.
5. Ward, 128.
6. Walter Wessel, "Romans," *The NIV Study Bible* (Grand Rapids, MI: Zondervan, 1985), 1724.

5 make bold I

LESSON FOUR

2 THESSALONIANS 2:10b-15

Truth and Consequences

In romantic relationships, there are many who love the chase more than the catch. The chase is full of idealism and potential; the catch is reality and accountability. The chase can be full of intense, fervent passion; the catch can be full of contentment and commitment that far outlast the chemical love potion that wears off within months. The chase can be thrilling, fun, challenging, energizing, and ego-enhancing; the catch can be stabilizing, fulfilling, demanding, and ego-submitting.

For these reasons and more, some people so prefer the chase that they avoid ever making a commitment to marriage. Or they enter into marriage without ever making a real commitment.

Many Christians at Thessalonica behaved that way toward the gospel of Christ. They loved the pursuit of truth, but not possessing it. They were always running after faddish theories and trendy teachers, but they never stood for truth, embraced the truth, or loved the truth.

Again, ask God to concentrate your focus for this study, not just to understand the truth, but to love the truth.

Top handwritten note:
If we say that we have fellowship with Him, and walk in darkness, we lie and do not practice the truth. 1 John 1:6

A powerful delusion (2:10b-12)

1. What attitude do some people have toward truth (see 2:10b)?

   That they did not receive the love of the truth, that they might be saved

2. a. How does God respond to those who do not love truth (see 2:11)?

   will be send them strong delusion that they should belive the lie,

   b. Why (see 2:12)?

   who did not believe the truth but had pleasure in unrighteousness,

---

The truth (2:10; also 13). Truth is most often associated with Jesus and the gospel (see John 8:32; 14:6; Romans 1:18; Galatians 2:5; Ephesians 1:13; 4:21; 1 John 1:6), which some people refused to love. Because they didn't love the gospel (truth), they did not obey Jesus' commands (see 1:8; compare Romans 2:8).

Left margin handwritten notes:
John 8:32 = "And you shall know the truth, and the truth shall make you free." 14:6 = Jesus said to him "I am the way, the truth, and the life. No one comes to the Father except through me." Galatians 2:5 - To whom we did not yield submission even for an hour, that the truth of the gospel might continue with you. Ephesians 1:13 - in Him you also trusted, after you heard the word of truth, the gospel of your salvation; in whom also, having believed, you were sealed with the Holy Spirit of promise (Col. 4:2?) if indeed you have heard Him and have been taught by Him as the truth is in Jesus.

Bottom handwritten notes:
He thanks Jesus Christ that your faith is spoken of throughout the whole world. 2:8 = but to those who are self seeking & do not obey the truth.

52

Powerful delusion (2:11). The delusion that God sends is likely a self-delusion or a product of their own willful thinking, as in Romans 1:24-28.

The lie (2:11). Not falsehood in general, but the specific lie that the man of lawlessness is divine (see 2:4).

Delighted in wickedness (2:12). More than passive dissent or intellectual skepticism, these people were actively engaged in moral error and in recruiting others to join them in their sin.

Study Skill—Cause and Effect
Language such as *for this reason*, *so that*, *because*, or *therefore* points to an explanation, an instrumental means, an effective cause, the purpose-in-mind, or the end-in-view. By observing this language of cause and effect, and by asking questions about it, we can discern the author's intent.

Biblical writers use language of cause and effect much more than secular writers of history, because they were given the theological reason why things happen. They want to impress on readers that events in sequence don't just "happen," but are caused by God for a purpose.

Language of cause and effect colors all biblical narratives so that every choice is construed as having a moral consequence, and so that the hand of God is perceived in everything that happens.

---

3. What step-by-step path do those who have "refused to love the truth" follow (see 2:10-12)?

that they may be saved God will send them strong delusion, that they should believe the lie: all may be condemned who did not believe the truth but had pleasure in unrighteousness.

Rom 16:19 - for your obedience has become known to all, He wants you to be wise in what is good, simple concerning evil.

Standing firm (2:13-15)

4. By contrast, what is the fate of those who "stand firm and hold fast to" the truth (2:15)?

Stand fast & hold the Traditions which you were taught weather by word or our epistle.

We ought always to thank God (2:13). Thanksgiving is not optional but is elicited from the recipients of God's love in action (see 1 Thessalonians 2:13-5:18). This note of thanksgiving resumes Paul's train of thought (see 2 Thessalonians 1:11-12) before his digression about the Antichrist (see 2:1-12).

God chose you as firstfruits (2:13). Election, from God's perspective, has no beginning, but is true eternally. "Firstfruits" could refer to Paul's Jewish converts at Thessalonica (see Acts 17:4), thus lending support to the theory that there were two churches there—one Gentile and one Jewish—to which 1 and 2 Thessalonians were written, respectively (see Introduction). More likely, these firstfruits refer to Paul's coworkers there.[1]

Sanctifying work (2:13). Sanctification is not optional or reserved for special Christians, but is mandated by God and accomplished through the Spirit working in the faith of those who are loved, saved (see 2:13), and called (see 2:14). Sanctification will be completed at the Second Coming (see 1 Thessalonians 5:23-24).

54

Our gospel (2:14). Means "good news," which originated with God, so it is the gospel of God (see Romans 1:1-2; 1 Thessalonians 2:8-9). This good news also involved Christ's work on the cross, so it is also the gospel of Christ (see 1 Thessalonians 3:2). And this same gospel is the one believed by and "passed on" by Paul, Silas, and Timothy, so it is rightly "our gospel."[2]

Stand firm (2:15; see also 1 Thessalonians 3:8). While an imperative, this command is not like talking to one lying down on the job ("Hop to it! Get to your feet!"), but comes with something secure to stand on—one's election, salvation, calling, and hope of glory—all secured by God in Christ. *Stand up for God,*

By word of mouth or by letter (2:15). The first apostolic mission at Thessalonica is in view here (see Acts 17:1) and perhaps return visits. Reference to a previous letter suggests that the present order of 1 and 2 Thessalonians (based on length) is also the chronological order (see Introduction). While that church no doubt preferred face-to-face visits with Paul and his associates, later generations of Christians can be grateful that such visits were not always convenient and that letters had to suffice, some of which have survived to this day.

5. What role does each person of the Trinity play in predestination, election, salvation, and sanctification (see 2:13-14; see also Romans 3; Galatians 5; Ephesians 1:3-14; Colossians 1:15-19; 2 Peter 1:1-11)?

Father *under obligation*
_____
_____
_____
_____

Rom 16:21
Timothy my fellow worker, & Lucius, Jason, & Sosipater, my kinsmen greet you;

Hold the tradition which you were taught whether by word or by an epistle.
1 Th 3:8 For now we live, if you stand fast in the Lord.

Son _____

_____

_____

_____

_____

Holy Spirit _____

_____

_____

_____

_____

6. What path toward glory do those who love
   the truth follow (see 2:14-15; see also Romans
   8:28-30)?

_____

_____

_____

_____

_____

Your response

7. Among your friends and acquaintances, who comes
   to mind when Paul speaks of people who have
   "refused to love the truth and so be saved" (2:10)?

_____

_____

_____

_____

_____

_____

_____

8. What can you lovingly say to that "unsaved" person this week that will bless and persuade your friend to stop delighting in wickedness, turn to God, and embrace the truth of the gospel?

_____

_____

_____

_____

_____

9. Paul is most grateful for his brothers and sisters at Thessalonica who stand firm in their faith and hold to the teachings he passed on to them. Among those you have influenced for Christ over the years, who comes to mind as one who holds steadfast to the Christian tradition in response to God's call, perhaps even as a tribute to your ministry in their life?

_____

_____

_____

_____

_____

_____

10. Is there any area in your life where you need to "stand firm" (2:15)? How will you do that?

_____

_____

_____

_____

_____

_____

11. What can you do to "hold fast to the teachings" (2:15) Paul gives in this section of 2 Thessalonians?

_____

_____

_____

_____

_____

For the group

Warm-up. Pick one of the following questions to begin your group discussion:

1. Who has been like a mentor in your spiritual life—someone who may have first discipled you or encouraged you with occasional visits and letters, so that you would stay true to what you first learned?
2. To whom have you been like a mentor—someone who has heeded your words of encouragement for their self-improvement, perhaps even their salvation and growth in Christ?
3. When did the "gospel of Christ" first become "my gospel"?

Discussion. After your individual study, come together as a group to share and confirm your understandings and biblical insights. Your goal is to cultivate a "love for truth" and to pay equal attention to what's going on with each member, some of whom may be under conviction.

Prayer. As a group, pray for those who have refused to love truth (question 7). Ask God to show you how to reach out to them. Finally, thank God for those who hold steadfastly to truth and are an encouragement to you.

1. F. F. Bruce, *1 & 2 Thessalonians* (Waco, TX: Word, 1982), 190.
2. Leon Morris, "1 & 2 Thessalonians," *The NIV Study Bible* (Grand Rapids, MI: Zondervan, 1985), 1821.

2 THESSALONIANS 2:16–3:5

Answers to Prayer

E. M. Bounds' 1911 classic *The Preacher and Prayer* (now *Purpose in Prayer*) may be summed up in these oft-quoted lines:

> We are constantly on a stretch if not a strain, to devise new methods, new plans, new organizations to advance the Church and secure enlargement and efficiency for the gospel. . . . Men are God's method. The Church is looking for better methods; God is looking for better men. . . . The Holy Ghost does not flow through methods, but through men. He does not come on machinery, but men. He does not anoint plans, but men—men of prayer.

Paul couldn't have said it any better. He prays for others and asks for prayer for himself and his associates. In concert with Paul and the Thessalonians, we can learn to become the kind of men and women of prayer that God wants us to be.

God's encouragement (2:16-17)

1. What is the difference between a prayer and a wish? (You may want to look the words up in a dictionary to help support your answer.)

we need to pray in Jesus' name, Paul is saying the free grace of God, Paul ask for prayer for them . . . that the word would be spread.

A prayer is a concern — a wish is something you would like, but don't need

61

When you pray always thanks God for the answer. Jesus want to hear from us. Ask the Holy Spirit, make a par

2. a. Is Paul expressing a prayer or a wish in 2:16-17?

Paul is a prayer

b. Why do you think so?

He asks God, Paul knows God is his helper, and God is the ruler over all things,

3. a. Compare 2:16-17 with 1 Thessalonians 3:11-13; 5:23. How are they similar?

That God would clear the way

b. How are they different?

Ask God to come + make a way for them.

When is ...recognize that the Lord Jesus Christ + our God + Father who has loved us + given us everlasting consolation + good hope by grace 2 Th 2:16 / and in 1 the 3:11 is asking God + Father himself + our Lord Jesus Christ direct...

Eternal encouragement (2:16). The Greek word *parakleesis*, here translated "encouragement," is eternal in the person of the Holy Spirit, known in John's gospel as *Paraclete*, translated the "Advocate" (NIV) or "Comforter" (KJV).

Encourage . . . strengthen (2:17). This prayer for inner courage (*parakaleo*) and strength draws from God, who is the eternal source of encouragement and hope.

Request for prayer (3:1-5)

4. What specific things do Paul and his coworkers pray for in 3:1-5?

Paul / he jm pray for them work, that that the word for the Lord may have free course be glorified, the Lord direct there hearts into the love of God.

Wicked (3:2). Literally, "out of place" or absurd. Elsewhere in the New Testament this word describes things rather than people. Paul is saying that evil is absurdly out of place, and has no business opposing the gospel.[1]

Not everyone has faith (3:2). Apart from the fact that not all people are Christians, Paul might be intimating that not all who claim to be Christians really have faith. This lack of faith in people, or people lacking faith in God, stands in sharp contrast to the faithfulness of the covenant-keeping, prayer-answering God (see 3:3). This contrast is made all the more sharp in

For Further Study: *or why To you,* What theological significance do you draw from the fact that Paul sometimes names God before Christ (see 1 Thessalonians 3:11), and other times Christ before God (see 2 Thessalonians 2:16)?

For Thought and Discussion: The apostles pray for the Word of God to increase and be honored (literally, "glorified"). Is this bibliolatry (worshiping a book as if it were God)? Why, or why not?

For Further Study: Paul wrote this letter from Corinth, where he stayed for a year and a half despite experiencing extreme difficulties. To learn more about Paul's experiences at Corinth, see Acts 18:6-17.

Worshiping Hd word not the book.

the Greek, where the words "faith" (*pistis*) and "faithful" (*pistos*) occur side by side (as the last word in verse 2 and the first of verse 3). Only those who place their faith in God know Him to be faithful.[2]

The Lord is faithful (3:3). This expression implies that God will never waiver in doing all that He has promised. Specifically, the covenant-keeping God faithfully keeps believers "firm to the end" (1 Corinthians 1:8), enables believers to "endure" temptation (1 Corinthians 10:13), fulfills all His promises and establishes the believer in Christ (see 2 Corinthians 1:18-21), and sanctifies believers in "spirit, soul and body" (1 Thessalonians 5:23). In the present context, the phrase functions like an "Amen!" to their prayers.

5. On what does Paul base his confidence (see 3:4)?

in the Soul

_____

_____

_____

_____

_____

Answers to Prayer

God is fully able (see Ephesians 3:20), eager (see Isaiah 65:24), and generous (see Jeremiah 33:3) to answer our prayers.

Our prayers may go unanswered or be hindered due to wickedness on our part (see Proverbs 15:29), an unforgiving or proud attitude (see Matthew 6:5-8,15), doubt (see James 1:5-8), lack of persistency (see Luke 11:5-13; 18:1-8), or wrong motives (see James 4:1-3).

Despite this, there are answers to prayer recorded in almost every book of the Bible.

- Moses' prayers for the Israelites' needs were answered with God's provision of manna, quail, and water in the wilderness (see Exodus 16–17).
- Hannah's prayers for a son were answered in Samuel, and five more children after him (see 1 Samuel 1–2).
- Solomon's prayers for wisdom were answered far beyond what he asked for (see 1 Kings 3:5-13; 4:29-34).
- Elijah's prayers for drought and then rain were answered (see James 5:17-18; 1 Kings 17:1; 18:36-46).
- Nehemiah's prayers to rebuild the walls of Jerusalem were answered as he overcame many obstacles (see Nehemiah 1:5-11; 2:5; 4:4-5,9; 6:9).
- Peter was delivered from prison, much to the amazement of those who prayed for his deliverance (see Acts 12:1-17).

For Thought and Discussion: What role does prayer play in the spiritual war against the Evil One? (Won't God do what He's going to do whether we pray or not?)

For Thought and Discussion: How does prayer "work"? (Does it change God's mind? Or does it only direct our hearts to desire His will? Does it change our outlook on circumstances or the circumstances themselves?) How does Paul support your view?

6. a. Are you confident that God will answer your prayers? Why?

yes, He said so.

b. How have you remained confident despite unanswered prayers?

keep praying and give God the glory for the answer to your Prayer. Keep praising Him

From the evil one (3:3). This expression, *tou poneerou*, can either refer to a person or a thing. It recalls the Lord's prayer (Matthew 6:13), "but deliver us from the evil one." This Evil One, or Satan, underlies the "evil people" (2 Thessalonians 3:2).

Strengthen you and protect you (3:3). Resisting evil requires both inner strengthening and outer guarding by God.

God's love and Christ's perseverance (3:5). The outpouring of God's love into people's hearts is to be reflected in their love for Him and others, especially as they identify with Christ's endurance of suffering (see Hebrews 12:1-2). People will gladly persevere despite suffering and evil when they are assured of God's love.

7. How does God direct the hearts of His people (see 3:5)?

PS. 37:4
He plants his will, the Lord is faithful, He will establish you and guard you from the evil one.

Your response

8. What area of prayer do you struggle with most? Pick one and explain why.

☐ How to talk with God so He'll listen.
☐ How to listen and discern what God is saying to me.
☐ Why God seems to answer some prayers and not others.
☐ How my prayers here make a difference for a missionary "over there".
☐ How to get past my "want list" and pray unselfishly for others.
☐ How to increase my "confidence in the Lord" (3:4) and believe Him for more.
☐ Trusting that "the Lord is faithful" (3:3), as I continue to struggle with sin.

☐ Reflecting "Christ's perseverance," as
I impatiently wait for answers.

☐ Other *I pray for others & things till*
I feel that God has answered them,
God is faithful to me

_____

_____

_____

_____

9. Where have you seen God's Word "spread
rapidly and be honored" (3:1), exalting Christ
and bringing people to faith?

Sept 9-11 when it happen. People prayed
and believe.

_____

_____

_____

_____

_____

_____

For the group

Warm-up. Begin this week's lesson by asking one
of the following questions:

1. What are the more persistent items on your
   evolving prayer list?
2. Name one answer to prayer you have received in
   recent months.
3. When did you first take God at His word and
   experience "the Lord is faithful"?

Discussion. After your individual study, come
together as a group to share and confirm your

2016 - 2/22
God answered my
prayer for Jennette.
thank you God.
you are so Great,
Love you God,

67

understandings and biblical insights. Your goal is to cultivate confidence in the Lord and to take each member's prayer concerns to God in prayer. Encourage each other by sharing your answers to question 9. What can you learn from each other's answers about how God works?

Prayer. Take time to share requests and pray specifically for one another the requests mentioned during the warm-up.

1. Leon Morris, "1 & 2 Thessalonians," *The NIV Study Bible* (Grand Rapids, MI: Zondervan, 1985), 1830; also F. F. Bruce, *1 & 2 Thessalonians* (Waco, TX: Word, 1982), 198.
2. Morris, 1830; also Bruce, 200.

2 THESSALONIANS 3:6-15

No Work, No Food

It's easy to feel frustrated by those around us who don't work and rely on others to support them. We become indignant, insisting that people should earn their own keep and work for what they need. Where does our value for work come from? Biblically speaking, this work-for-food ethic is rooted and reflected in principles put forth by the apostle Paul to the "idle busybodies" at Thessalonica who were living off the welfare of conscientious workers.

Ask God to concentrate your focus for this study, on your own and as a group, especially its application to workers and non-workers alike.

The sin of not working (3:6-10)

1. How should we treat those within the church who are idle or lazy (see 3:6)?

With draw from every brother who walks disorderly and not according to the tradition which he received from us

2. What gives Paul the authority to speak boldly
about this subject (see 3:7-9)?

by make themselves an example

3. What kind of example did Paul provide the church
at Thessalonica in regard to work (see 3:7-9)?

They did not eat any bred.
Free, but worked for it ,

Matt 18:17- And if he
refuses to hear them
tell it to the church.
But if he refuses
even to hear the church
let him be to you like a
heather and a tax collector.
4:11-12: mind your own
business, work with your
hands + that you may
walk properly to those
outside / 5:14- Comfort
the faint hearted, uphold the
weak, be patient with all
4:1-8- he who rejects this does
not rejected man, but God,
who has also given us His
Holy Spirit)
Follow Pauls command

Keep away (3:6; compare verse 14). The principle of
shunning or isolating another person is at work
here. That meant some privileges and associa-
tions of intimate fellowship, perhaps even the
Lord's Supper or the sharing of needs, were to
be withheld from a person, but the shunned
person was not cut off from all contact. People
who were shunned were not treated as enemies
but as brothers and sisters (see 3:15).

The teaching you received from us (3:6). This
could be the teaching Paul gave in his first letter
regarding idleness (see 1 Thessalonians 4:11-12;
5:14) or about holy living that pleases God (see
4:1-8).

Follow our example (3:7). Paul frequently urges
others to imitate him, just as all believers are to
imitate godly leaders (see 3:9; 1 Timothy 4:12;
Titus 2:7). This gives leaders the responsibility
to be imitators of Christ (see 1 Corinthians 11:1;
Ephesians 4:32–5:11; 1 Thessalonians 1:6).

70 *Be a example to the believer*
in word in conduct in love

We were not idle (3:7). Literally, "we were not out of order." The Greek verb *atakteo*, in the military context, speaks of loss of morale, irregular discipline, disorderly conduct, and desertion.[1]

4. How would you describe Paul's attitude toward these idle brothers and sisters? (Is he being fair? Mean-spirited? Pastoral? Preachy? Brotherly?)

He wanted them to follow them believe in Jesus. Yes / he cared for them,

Work to eat

For Thought and Discussion: Some people are so heavenly-minded that they are no earthly good. They see work on earth as unnecessary and unimportant. Since God's people will work in heaven (see Isaiah 65:17-25; Revelation 15:1-4; 22:1-11), how important is it to work on earth?

5. Why do you suppose Paul refused financial help in Thessalonica, even though he had this apostolic right (see 3:8-9)?

He wanted to show them how to labore for their food, don't be idle. be busie. He did not want to be a burden to anyone

The right to such help (3:9). On other occasions, Paul exerted his apostolic right to receive support from those he ministered to (see Philippians 4:15). But here at Thessalonica, Paul called his reader's attention to his self-supporting lifestyle, one that was not a burden or financial liability, but a model of diligence (see 2 Thessalonians 3:7-9; Acts 18:3; 1 Thessalonians 4:11-12; 5:14).

The one who is unwilling to work shall not eat (3:10). The pagan forms of this rule were stated as platitudes: "He who does not work does not eat."[2] Contemporary Jewish teaching cites Rabbi

Abbahu as saying, "If I do not work, I do not eat." The second-century Christian work, *The Didache*, instructs Christians on a related rule of hospitality, that travelers could and should be given a three-day provision, and if they stay longer they should use their craft: "Let him work for his bread, . . . so that no one shall live with you in idleness as a Christian."[3] Paul states his rule as a command to be obeyed.

Discipline and blessing (3:11-15)

6. a. Does Paul expect full compliance with his instructions and commands in this matter of idle busybodies and church discipline (see 3:14-15)?

_____

_____

_____

_____

b. What would be most difficult about following through on the sanctions that Paul has imposed on the brothers and sisters who live off others?

_____

_____

_____

_____

Busybodies (3:11). Worse than idle, these people involved themselves in other people's affairs and stirred up trouble.

Doing what is good (3:13). Some Thessalonians were in danger of losing their zeal for God.

72

They needed the encouragement and example of Paul, as well as the grace and peace that come from God (see 3:16,18) in order to continue doing good. In a religion of grace, good works flow from—but do not contribute to—salvation.

Do not associate with them (3:14). See notes at verse 6. The sanctions of 1 Corinthians 5:9-11, by comparison, were a more severe form of social isolation, akin to formal excommunication.

Warn them as you would a fellow believer (3:15). The language here describes a close family relationship between believers. The concept is not a mere sentiment, but contains stern warnings predicated on the principle of mutual accountability for the purpose of restoring the wayward to their senses (see Galatians 6:1).

Your response

7. What aspect of work do you struggle with most? Pick one and explain why.

☐ I don't work outside the home, but I feel I should be "earning" my way.
☐ I work outside the home, but wish others could support me.
☐ I am a hard worker, but often neglect my family.
☐ I withdrew from the rat race, and I'm far behind "those who made it."
☐ I've maintained upward vocational mobility in the pursuit of success.
☐ I let myself be passed up by others; now I may be vulnerable to layoffs.
☐ I need to trust that the Lord will provide a suitable job for me.
☐ I've put in my time (twenty or thirty years); now it's my turn to live off others.
☐ I can't afford to retire, and never will, because I refuse to be a burden to my kids.
☐ I don't like to see loafers on the job getting as much as I do.
☐ I've picked up some bad work habits from idle, lazy people around me.

Optional Application: Do you prefer to follow a command or an example at work? Why?

Optional Application: Suppose you were given the job of heading up and enforcing Paul's "Work-to-Eat Program." What would you do to ensure its success?

☐ Other: _____
_____
_____
_____

8. a. Can you see Paul making any exceptions to his "no work, no food" rule? For whom?
_____
_____
_____
_____

b. What exceptions would you make for situations or people you know about?
_____
_____
_____
_____

c. What kind of help do you think should be given to people who do not work?
_____
_____
_____
_____

74

9. Paul says to avoid those brothers and sisters who are idle. How should we as Christians treat those who are idle outside the church?

_____

_____

_____

_____

_____

_____

_____

Optional Application: How does your church, denomination, or Christian organization exercise spiritual discipline in matters relating to work and the duty to provide for one's own family?

For the group

Warm-up. Pick one of the questions below to begin this week's study:

1. What one good work habit did you pick up from your father or mother?
2. What one good work habit would you like your kid(s) to pick up from you?

Discussion. Many people have strong feelings about those who don't work, yet receive government support. As you work through this week's lesson, try to look beyond your own feelings on the subject to see how God wants you to respond. Pay special attention to question 9 as you seek understanding about this controversial subject.

Prayer. Thank God for your jobs and pray for those who are out of work or unable to work. Ask Him to show your group how to minister to those people outside the church who do not work to support themselves or their families.

Service opportunity. Volunteer as a group to work at a local soup kitchen or homeless shelter. Often putting faces and names to general groups of people (welfare recipients, the homeless) can give us new insight into an issue or problem.

1. F. F. Bruce, *1 & 2 Thessalonians* (Waco, TX: Word, 1982), 205.
2. Leon Morris, "1 & 2 Thessalonians," *The NIV Study Bible* (Grand Rapids, MI: Zondervan, 1985), 1830.
3. Bruce, 206.

2 THESSALONIANS 3:16-18

Final Words and Review

Final words

1. What is the significance of Paul writing this benediction himself (see 3:17)?

_____

_____

_____

_____

_____

2. Paul ends his letter to the Thessalonians with a blessing of grace and peace. Why would the Thessalonians need these two things (see 3:16,18)?

Grace _____

_____

_____

_____

Peace _____

_____

_____

_____

_____

_____

I, Paul, write this greeting (3:17). See Introduction. Paul customarily dictated his letters, but always added a personal greeting, benediction, or trademark signature at the close of each letter (see 1 Corinthians 16:21; Galatians 6:11; Colossians 4:18).

Review

3. Reread 2 Thessalonians. What are the most important lessons you learned from this study about:

Thanksgiving? _____

_____

_____

_____

_____

Prayer? _____

_____

_____

_____

_____

_____

_____

The Lord's return? _____

_____

_____

_____

_____

_____

Perseverance? _____

_____

_____

_____

_____

_____

Work? _____

_____

_____

_____

_____

_____

Other key lessons? _____

_____

_____

_____

_____

_____

_____

_____

_____

4. Scan through 2 Thessalonians once more. Do you have any questions that are still unanswered? If so, some of the sources on pages 83–87 may help you answer them. Or, you might want to study some particular passages with cross-references of your own.

_____

_____

_____

_____

_____

5. Have you changed as a result of studying 2 Thessalonians? (It might be an attitude, an opinion, a thought, or a relationship with another person.) How?

_____

_____

_____

_____

_____

6. Look back over your study of 2 Thessalonians, focusing on those sections where you expressed a desire to make some personal application. Are you satisfied with the way you have followed through? Take some time to pray about those areas you think you should continue to pursue. Make note of any resolutions about the future below.

_____

_____

For the group

Allow anyone in the group to ask any questions he or she may still have about 2 Thessalonians. Others in the group can respond to such questions if they have any insights or answers. If any question remains unanswered, make plans for someone to check one of the sources on pages 83–87 for insights that might help. The results can be shared at the next meeting.

At this point, you may want to evaluate how well your group functioned during your study of 2 Thessalonians. Questions you might ask include:

- What did you learn about small-group study?
- Were the needs of individual members met on a regular basis? (If there was any failure in this, what changes can be made in the group to improve the situation for future meetings?)
- Was everyone able to share their ideas with the rest of the group?
- Was your group prayer time fruitful?
- What will you do next as a group (take a break, have a party, study something new)?

STUDY AIDS

For further information on the material covered in this study, consider the following sources. If your local bookstore does not have them, ask the bookstore to order them from the publishers, or you can find them in a public university or seminary library. If they are out of print, you might be able to find them online.

Commentaries on 2 Thessalonians

Bruce, F. F. *1 & 2 Thessalonians* (Word, 1982).
    This leading evangelical scholar has made a valuable contribution to the Word Biblical Commentary series. He carefully explains Paul's theology in the context of the first-century church.

Milligan, George. *St. Paul's Epistles to the Thessalonians: The Greek Text with Introduction and Notes* (Eerdmans, 1952).
    This standard work is widely used to study 1 and 2 Thessalonians.

Morris, Leon. *The First and Second Epistles to the Thessalonians: The English Text with Introduction, Exposition and Notes* (Eerdmans, 1959).
    This volume in the New International Commentary series is a complete and full-scale study of Paul's letters to the Thessalonians.

Ward, Ronald. *Commentary on 1 & 2 Thessalonians* (Word, 1973).
    This commentary makes plain the meaning of the Greek text for those who have not studied the original biblical languages.

Historical and background sources

Bruce, F. F. *New Testament History* (Doubleday, 1979).
    A readable history of Herodian kings, Roman governors, philosophical schools, Jewish sects, Jesus, the early Jerusalem church, Paul,

and early Gentile Christianity. Well documented with footnotes for the serious student, but the notes do not intrude.

Harrison, E. F. *Introduction to the New Testament* (Eerdmans, 1971).
History from Alexander the Great—who made Greek culture dominant in the biblical world—through philosophies, pagan and Jewish religions, Jesus' ministry and teaching (the weakest section), and the spread of Christianity. Very good maps and photographs of the land, art, and architecture of New Testament times.

Packer, James I., Merrill C. Tenney, and William White, Jr. *The Bible Almanac* (Thomas Nelson, 1980).
One of the most accessible handbooks of the people of the Bible and how they lived. Many photos and illustrations liven an already readable text.

Histories, concordances, dictionaries, and handbooks

A **concordance** lists words of the Bible alphabetically along with each verse in which the word appears. It lets you do your own word studies. An *exhaustive* concordance lists every word used in a given translation, while an *abridged* or *complete* concordance omits either some words, some occurrences of the word, or both.

Two of the three best exhaustive concordances are the venerable *Strong's Exhaustive Concordance* and *Young's Analytical Concordance to the Bible*. Both are available based on the King James Version and the New American Standard Bible. *Strong's* has an index in which you can find out which Greek or Hebrew word is used in a given English verse (although its information is occasionally outdated). *Young's* breaks up each English word it translates. Neither concordance requires knowledge of the original languages.

Perhaps the best exhaustive concordance currently on the market is *The NIV Exhaustive Concordance*. It features a Hebrew-to-English and a Greek-to-English lexicon (based on the eclectic text underlying the NIV), which are also keyed to *Strong's* numbering system.

Among other good, less expensive concordances, *Cruden's Complete Concordance* is keyed to the King James and Revised Versions, the *NIV Complete Concordance* is keyed to the New International Version. These include all references to every word included, but they omit "minor" words. They also lack indexes to the original languages.

A **Bible dictionary** or **Bible encyclopedia** alphabetically lists articles about people, places, doctrines, important words, customs, and geography of the Bible.
The New Bible Dictionary edited by J. D. Douglas, F. F. Bruce, J. I. Packer, N. Hillyer, D. Guthrie, A. R. Millard, and D. J. Wiseman (Tyndale, 1982) is more comprehensive than most dictionaries. Its 1,300 pages include

84

quantities of information along with excellent maps, charts, diagrams, and an index for cross-referencing.

Unger's Bible Dictionary by Merrill F. Unger (Moody, 1979) is equally good and is available in an inexpensive paperback edition.

The Zondervan Pictorial Encyclopedia edited by Merrill C. Tenney (Zondervan, 1975, 1976) is excellent and exhaustive, and has been revised and updated. Its five 1,000-page volumes represent a significant financial investment, however, and all but very serious students may prefer to use it at a church, public college, or seminary library.

Unlike a Bible dictionary in the above sense, *Vine's Expository Dictionary of New Testament Words* by W. E. Vine (various publishers) alphabetically lists major words used in the King James Version and defines each New Testament Greek word that the KJV translates with its English word. *Vine's* also lists verse references where that Greek word appears, so you can do your own cross-references and word studies without knowing any Greek.

Vine's is a good, basic book for beginners, but it is much less complete than other Greek helps for English speakers. More serious students might prefer *The New International Dictionary of New Testament Theology* edited by Colin Brown (Zondervan) or *The Theological Dictionary of the New Testament* by Gerhard Kittel and Gerhard Friedrich, abridged in one volume by Geoffrey W. Bromiley (Eerdmans).

A **Bible atlas** can be a great aid to understanding what is going on in a book of the Bible and how geography affected events. Here are a few good choices:

The Macmillan Atlas by Yohanan Aharoni and Michael Avi-Yonah (Macmillan, 1968, 1977) contains 264 maps, 89 photos, and 12 graphics. The many maps of individual events portray battles, movements of people, and changes of boundaries in detail.

The New Bible Atlas by J. J. Bimson and J. P. Kane (Tyndale, 1985) has 73 maps, 34 photos, and 34 graphics. Its evangelical perspective, concise and helpful text, and excellent research make it a very good choice, but its greatest strength lies in outstanding graphics, such as cross-sections of the Dead Sea.

The Bible Mapbook by Simon Jenkins (Lion, 1984) is much shorter and less expensive than most other atlases, so it offers a good first taste of the usefulness of maps. It contains 91 simple maps, very little text, and 20 graphics. Some of the graphics are computer-generated and intriguing.

The Moody Atlas of Bible Lands by Barry J. Beitzel (Moody, 1984) is scholarly, evangelical, and full of theological text, indexes, and references. This admirable reference work will be too deep and costly for some, but Beitzel shows vividly how God prepared the land of Israel perfectly for the acts of salvation He planned to accomplish in it.

A **handbook** of biblical customs can also be useful. Two good ones are *Today's Handbook of Bible Times and Customs* by William L. Coleman (Bethany, 1984) and the less detailed *Daily Life in Bible Times* (Nelson, 1982).

For small-group leaders

Barker, Steve, et al. *The Small Group Leader's Handbook* (InterVarsity, 1982).
Written by an InterVarsity small group with college students primarily in mind. It includes information on small-group dynamics and how to lead in light of them, and many ideas for worship, building community, and outreach. It has a good chapter on doing inductive Bible study.

Griffin, Em. *Getting Together: A Guide for Good Groups* (InterVarsity, 1982).
Applies to all kinds of groups, not just Bible studies. From his own experience, Griffin draws deep insights into why people join groups; how people relate to each other; and principles of leadership, decision making, and discussions. It is fun to read, but its 229 pages will take more time than the above book.

Hunt, Gladys. *You Can Start a Bible Study Group* (Harold Shaw, 1984).
Builds on Hunt's thirty years of experience leading groups. This book is wonderfully focused on God's enabling. It is both clear and applicable for Bible study groups of all kinds.

McBride, Neal F. *How to Build a Small Groups Ministry* (NavPress, 1994).
This hands-on workbook for pastors and lay leaders includes everything you need to know to develop a plan that fits your unique church. Through basic principles, case studies, and worksheets, McBride leads you through twelve logical steps for organizing and administering a small-groups ministry.

McBride, Neal F. *How to Lead Small Groups* (NavPress, 1990).
Covers leadership skills for all kinds of small groups—Bible study, fellowship, task, and support groups. Filled with step-by-step guidance and practical exercises to help you grasp the critical aspects of small-group leadership and dynamics.

Bible study methods

Braga, James. *How to Study the Bible* (Multnomah, 1982).
Clear chapters on a variety of approaches to Bible study: synthetic, geographical, cultural, historical, doctrinal, practical, and so on. Designed to help the ordinary person without seminary training to use these approaches.

Fee, Gordon, and Douglas Stuart. *How to Read the Bible for All Its Worth* (Zondervan, 1982).
After explaining in general what interpretation and application are, Fee and Stuart offer chapters on interpreting and applying the different kinds of writing in the Bible: Epistles, Gospels, Old Testament Law, Old

Testament narrative, the Prophets, Psalms, Wisdom, and Revelation. Fee and Stuart also suggest good commentaries on each biblical book. They write as evangelical scholars who personally recognize Scripture as God's Word for their daily lives.

Jensen, Irving L. *Independent Bible Study* (Moody, 1963), and *Enjoy Your Bible* (Moody, 1962).
The former is a comprehensive introduction to the inductive Bible study method, especially the use of synthetic charts. The latter is a simpler introduction to the subject.

Wald, Oletta. *The Joy of Discovery in Bible Study* (Augsburg, 1975).
Wald focuses on issues such as how to observe all that is in a text, how to ask questions of a text, how to use grammar and passage structure to see the writer's point, and so on. Very helpful on these subjects.

Encounter God's Word
Experience LifeChange
LifeChange by The Navigators

The LifeChange Bible study series can help you grow in Christ-likeness through a life-changing encounter with God's Word. Discover what the Bible says, and develop the skills and desire to dig even deeper into God's Word. Each study includes study aids and discussion questions.

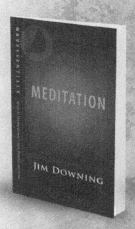 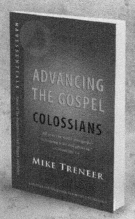 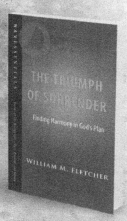

The *Message* Means Understanding

Bringing the Bible to all ages

he Message is written in contemporary language that is much like talking with a good friend. When paired with your favorite Bible study, *The Message* will deliver a reading experience that is reliable, energetic, and amazingly fresh.

SUPPORT THE MINISTRY OF THE NAVIGATORS

The Navigators' calling is to advance the gospel of Jesus and His kingdom into the nations through spiritual generations of laborers living and discipling among the lost.

Navigators have invested their lives in people for more than 75 years, coming alongside them life on life to help them passionately know Christ and to make Him known.

The U.S. Navigators' ministry touches lives in varied settings, including college campuses, military bases, downtown offices, urban neighborhoods, prisons, and youth camps.

Dedicated to helping people navigate spiritually, The Navigators aims to make a permanent difference in the lives of people around the world. The Navigators helps its communities of friends to follow Christ passionately and equip them effectively to go out and do the same.

To learn more about donating to The Navigators' ministry, go to **www.navigators.org/us/support** or call toll-free at **1-866-568-7827**.